Advance Praise

"If you are ready to kick the 'CAN'TS' out of your life now, read, think about, absorb, and use the brilliance in my friend Steve Gottry's book. Make new positivity the adventurous journey into a bigger, brighter, and more exciting future than you have ever imagined!"

—**MARK VICTOR HANSEN**
Co-creator and Co-author of the
Chicken Soup For The Soul series.
Co-author (with Crystal Dwyer Hansen) of *ASK!*

"I'm a raving fan of Steve Gottry. He's one of the most caring, loving, and insightful human beings I know. Read *The Thirteen "You Can'ts"* and reduce frustration in your life and begin to experience the life you were supposed to live."

—**KEN BLANCHARD**
Coauthor of *The One Minute Manager*
and Co-Editor of *Servant Leadership In Action*

"It's probably not the most admirable trait, but I think it's natural for all of us to go through life with a bit of built-in skepticism. So, when I picked up Steve Gottry's manuscript for *The Thirteen "You Can'ts,"* I was prepared to question 'this and that.'

"What a pleasant, unexpected surprise! I found myself agreeing with every key point he made. I fully agree that our lives will be more rewarding if we learn to accept the things we can't change, and focus on the things we CAN.

"This concept reminds me of the wise prayer written by the American theologian Reinhold Niebuhr (1892–1971):

'God, grant me the serenity to accept the things I cannot change, the courage to change the things I can, and the wisdom to know the difference.'

"I believe this slim volume will help you speak those words . . . and MEAN them."

—**COLLEEN BARRETT**
President Emeritus of Southwest Airlines
Co-author (with Ken Blanchard) of *Lead With Luv*

"Steve Gottry left out the 14th You Can't: Since he overlooked this, I'll fill it in for him: the 14th You Can't is: 'YOU CAN'T PUT THIS BOOK DOWN.' The book is an amazing combination of enlightening and compelling."

—**MITZI PERDUE (MRS. FRANK PERDUE)**
Author, Businesswoman, and Founder:
Win This Fight, Stop Human Trafficking Now!
Author of *How To Make Your Family Business Last*,
How To Communicate Values To Children,
and *How To Keep Your Family Connected*.

"When I first picked this book up, it honestly triggered my ego because I thought, 'I can do anything as a Navy SEAL, right!?' But as I allowed myself to get past my beliefs, I realized Steve is onto something that is rarely, if ever spoken of: finding what you can't do will help you craft a life by your design that you *can* do. It is critical to be honest with yourself and understand your limits to understand your ability to achieve your potential. I encourage you to open your mind, absorb these words, and rethink what you may already believe."

—**BRIAN "IRON ED" HINER**
USN SEAL (Retired) Iraq · Afghanistan · Philippines
Bestselling author of *First Fast Fearless* and *Guts*

"Steve's insights are humorous, real, and exactly what we all need to hear. In a world that tells us there is no such thing as 'impossible,' that premise simply isn't true. You can lead a horse to water, but you can't make him drink. We are responsible 'to' people not 'for' people. It's okay to let people fail. The only people we can change are ourselves. These truths, and so many more, are found in the pages of Steve's book. If my father were alive today, he'd summarize the message like this: 'I am what I am, and I ain't what I ain't, and I'm still tremendous!'"

—DR. TRACEY JONES, MBA, PH.D.
(Daughter of Charlie "Tremendous" Jones)
President of Tremendous Leadership
Author of *Beyond Tremendous*,
Raising the Bar On Life: A Message To Millennials;
and *SPARK: 5 Essentials to Ignite the Greatness Within*

"Thanks for inviting me to be among the first to read *The Thirteen "You Can'ts."* It was an easy read, and it was fun! I was amazed at how many of the 'thirteen' I knew and agreed with.

"Many were the things I learned from my folks, my religious instruction classes, and a few enlightened teachers that I had filed away under 'bits and pieces of wisdom and commonsense.'

"As I read your book, the contents of that file came back to me in your non-preachy, light-hearted style of writing."

—DALE MENTEN
Past Billboard "Hot 100" Composer/Arranger/Musician

"This is a fabulous book, and something I felt driven to finish once I started it!

"It is a very well-written 'self-help book' from a different angle and should appeal to—and help—people who are hesitant to pick up a traditional book of this type. I love the way you pull everything together and give positives that we can focus on once we are able to accept the things we can't do. The amount of grief we put on ourselves over things out of our control gets overwhelming sometimes.

"I know several people I think could certainly benefit from reading this. Looking forward to being able to order some copies. Hopefully soon!"

—DAVD NELSON, A.J.P. OWNER AND FOUNDER
Nelson Estate Jewelers
www.nelsonestatejewelers.com

"Knowing what you really can't do allows you to fling all your energies and resources into what you can do. This is the critical take-away from this important and useful book. Read it, understand it, apply it, resculpt your life logistics and prepare for success. Thank you, Steve!"

—RABBI DANIEL LAPIN
From the Foreword

The
Thirteen
"You Can'ts"

The Thirteen "You Can'ts"

How to Discover,
Understand, and Accept
Your Impossibilities . . .
and Still Love Your Life!

Steve Gottry

MEDIA

Published 2022 by Gildan Media LLC
aka G&D Media
www.GandDmedia.com

Front Cover design by David Rheinhardt of Pyrographx

Interior design by Meghan Day Healey of Story Horse, LLC

Library of Congress Cataloging-in-Publication Data is available upon request

ISBN: 978-1-7225-0605-6

10   9   8   7   6   5   4   3   2   1

To all the well-meaning people—from the moment of my birth through today—who have tried to change me, revise me, control me, tell me what to think and do, and otherwise mess with my life.

❄ ❄ ❄

I'm sorry that you wasted all that precious time trying to do the impossible. Think instead about working on your own lives. I'm fine.

❄ ❄ ❄

Seriously, this book is dedicated to those wise people who "live and let live." Thank you for allowing the rest of us to live our lives!

❄ ❄ ❄

(This is from the "Almost-Libertarian" side of me.)

Contents

Foreword

by Rabbi Daniel Lapin

Virginia Oliver, may she live and be healthy, sets out in her lobster boat every day from June to September in order to tend her two hundred traps. She tackles the not-always-friendly waters of Rockland, Maine together with her seventy-eight-year-old son, Max. At the time of my writing this foreword for Steve's important and useful book, Virginia is 101.

Did her granddaughter ever say, "Granny, you can't take the boat out today, it's blowing twenty-five knots?" Did a healthcare advisor ever say, "Virginia, you can't lobster today, it's raining and you could fall and break a leg on the slippery deck of that old boat?" Actually, I have no idea. But what I do know is that Virginia never listened to anyone who told her, "You can't."

I admire Virginia. Yet, this is a book about how valuable it is to recognize the things you just can't do. What is more, it is a book that I have termed both important and useful. Many things are important but not useful. The Nagorno-Karabakh conflict between Armenia and Azerbaijan is certainly important in geopolitical terms but knowing about it can hardly be called useful. On the other hand, knowing how to rip a long-tenured bandage off your arm without a yelp of pain as you tear out dozens of hair follicles is certainly useful but is not really important.

The Thirteen "You Can'ts" is important because it shines an incandescent beam of brilliant light on a critical aspect of how we're created. Most animals on this amazingly varied planet prefer to avoid confrontation even when the rewards of victory would be substantial. Fight is preferable to flight only when escape is impossible. However, humans will face great risk for possible high reward or even sometimes nothing more than the reward of achievement.

There are top rate sales professionals who accept commission only positions. They confidently confront the risk of zero income in exchange for almost limitless upside potential. There are mountaineers like Ed Viesturs who has climbed all fourteen world peaks of more than 25,000 feet and climbers like Alex Honnold who climbed the cliff face of El Capitan in California's

Yosemite Park alone and without ropes. There are no animals that voluntarily place themselves at serious risk of bodily harm or death for no tangible reward.

Having been touched by the Divine, we humans find the allure of the unlimited to be all but irresistible. We obviously lack God's omniscience and His omnipotence but we sure seem to yearn for it. Even animals that store away food, as squirrels do, only store away the finite amounts needed to see them through the winter. Only humans possess a desire for wealth beyond the needs of a normal lifetime.

Many individuals expend immeasurable energy on the quest for power. Being able to exert control over others is for many, highly seductive. One need only observe with deserved dismay the extent to which government bureaucrats relish wielding power over citizen supplicants. Again, it is all but impossible to find similar behavior among animals.

Whether it is unlimited power, money or any of the other human appetites for which we yearn in limitless quantity, that yearning is a reflection of our Divine origins. Many people, in particular children who have not yet been bludgeoned by the vicissitudes of life, find the words "You can't" to be an almost irresistible trigger to try . . . Whether it is the child pushing at his parentally set limits or the athlete stirred to higher effort and achievement by a friend saying, "You couldn't do that" we all find ourselves vexed by any external efforts to impose limits upon ourselves.

There is obviously both a positive side to this as well as a negative aspect. Finding ourselves stimulated to greater effort and achievement by the gnawing irritant inside of ourselves that whispers, "Go on, you can do it. There's nothing you can't do" is clearly at the heart of unimaginable feats like Usain Bolt winning the 100 meters at the 2012 London Olympics in a blistering nine and a half seconds or a teenaged Khatia Buniatishvili playing Rachmaninov's demanding 2nd piano concerto in international competition.

The negative side of this allure of the infinite from which we humans suffer is the terrible danger of someone with the build of a compact refrigerator and a complete lack of natural talent being told that he could achieve the artistic heights of ballet dancing. He would sadly waste his life or valuable parts thereof in a quite futile attempt to overcome the whispered "You can't" when that is exactly the voice he should have attended.

And this is why Steve's book that you now hold in your hands is not only important but also useful. That heavily-built young man was never going to become the next Baryshnikov of the Kirov Ballet but he might well have achieved excellence in another field had he not wasted his years dreaming of dancing.

Bookshelves groan beneath the burden of the countless books speaking lyrically of hope and optimism. Believe in it and you'll be able to do it, they urge. And there are times most of us urgently need this kind of encouragement. Yes, there are many occasions on which we need to be reminded that many of our obstacles are mental and can be overcome by changing our thinking. Everyone can find a book along these lines that will match his mood.

But this important and useful book stands almost alone in emphasizing that we humans all do have certain limits and that learning what they are liberates us to reach for the sky in other areas.

In May 1954 British medical student, Roger Bannister, became the first human being to run a mile in under four minutes. Some doctors had confidently predicted that even the effort would kill an athlete. After Bannister breasted the tape in 3:59 on that blustery day in Oxford, he fell exhausted to the grass and commentators assumed he had died. They were wrong. Not only did he go on to break his own record a few months later but he enjoyed a long career as a successful doctor.

There was really nothing magical about a four-minute mile that should have alarmed some doctors into mistakenly assuming that it was impossible any more than some experts earlier assuming that a five-minute mile was impossible. But I assuredly inform you that no human being will ever run a one-minute mile just as I assert that no Olympic high jumper will ever jump unassisted over a two-story house. The reason is because objective measures having to do with things like human metabolism and gravity, reliably set those limits.

In other words, many challenges can be overcome by ignoring naysayers and refusing to hear the words "you can't." But wise people abandon those other challenges that truly can't be done. One can hardly overestimate the importance of being able to know the difference. Knowing what you really can't do allows you to fling all your energies and resources into what you can do. This is the critical take-away from this important and useful book. Read it, understand it, apply it, resculpt your life logistics and prepare for success. Thank you, Steve!

Rabbi Daniel Lapin is the Founder of the American Alliance of Jews and Christians, and the author of *Business Secrets from the Bible*. For his blogs and other information please see www.RabbiDanielLapin.com

Introduction

I admit it. I'm a hardcore junkie.

It's not about drugs. Or porn. Or cigarettes.

I'm addicted to "self-help" books. Videos. Seminars. Almost anything about any area of my life that I could possibly improve.

I have not read them all. No one could . . . it's a huge library.

But I've read Napoleon Hill's *Think and Grow Rich*, Dr. Norman Vincent Peale's *The Power of Positive Thinking*, Dr. Ken Blanchard and Dr. Peale's *The Power of Ethical Management*, and Dr. Robert Schuler's *If It's Going to Be, It's Up to Me*. I've read books by Wayne Dyer and Deepak Choprah, Dr. Denis Waitley, Zig Ziglar, and that guy who hugs everyone. I've read the Bible, arguably the greatest self-help book of all time. In fact, about the only thing I've missed out on is Phil McGraw. (Sorry, Dr. Phil.)

These books all have one thing in common. They tell the reader—you and me—what is possible, if you or I want it, seek it, work for it, pray for it, and believe in it.

What they DON'T tell us—for the most part, in most cases—is that there are things that we CAN'T do—no matter how fervently we want, seek, work, pray, or believe.

These things are the "can'ts." They are life's impossibilities. They are the things we will not accomplish . . . the rewards we will never realize.

I learned about my first "you can't" when I was a young boy—perhaps seven or eight years old. "Even if you put on a red cape and wear your underwear on the outside of your blue jeans, you are not Superman. You can't fly." My mother reminded me of that fact when she picked my bruised body up off the ground. (I found this to be particularly annoying, since she was the one who sewed the red cape for me on her Singer sewing machine in the first place.)

One quick mindless jump off the stairway that led to the second floor of our garage in Henderson, Minnesota, taught me that valuable lesson. As a result, I won't even jump out of a perfectly functioning airplane with a parachute. Let alone without one. I simply can't fly.

Over the years, I've discovered a number of other significant "you can'ts." A while back, I learned one from Ron White, the Blue-Collar-Tour comedian: "You can't fix stupid." How true that is! Stupid abounds in the world today. From business, to city halls, to state capitals, to Washington, D.C., there is so little about our society that makes sense to me. (I sometimes wonder if this is deliberate!)

I've also learned that I can't get anyone else to adopt my positions on anything, no matter how much I talk, write, or blog. I finally realized that a Facebook post is unlikely to change anyone's mind about anything.

It ain't easy to accept these unpleasant limitations. But, in thinking about them, I've concluded that there are actually only thirteen significant ones.

These thirteen "can'ts" are deceptively simple. They are also simply deceptive. Most of us, in failing to achieve them, feel that we have been defeated by events and circumstances that we should have been able to control.

That, friends, is rubbish. It's a lie. The problem has nothing to do with our inability to control things around us, and everything to do with how we deal with, and eventually accept, what we can do and can't do.

This book is about living your own life in contentment, by moving beyond your expectations and limitations.

This book is designed to be a huge, overwhelming breath of fresh air that will help you experience freedom as you've never known it. Until now.

When you reach the last page, you may say to yourself, "I knew all that." But did you really? Do you live your life as though you had known "all that?" Are you willing to let go? Are you willing to move on? Are you ready to love your life AGAIN? Or STILL? Or MORE?

By discovering, understanding, and accepting these thirteen limitations, you will be free to maximize your personal potential in ways you never imagined possible. You will live your own life, rather than trying to live the lives of those you know and love. Still, in the process of discovery, you may also find subtle, simple ways to help those you love.

Let's discover the thirteen "you cant's" together.

Oh, one more thing. I love you! ALL of you! I really do!

one

You Can't Read the Minds of Others.

We've all heard stories about "mind readers," clairvoyants, or psychics who can somehow see the unseen, hear the unheard, know the unknown, and read minds . . . not to mention predict the future.

I really don't know if there is any valid scientific research behind this phenomenon, although I am personally acquainted with a woman who is called upon by the local sheriff's office on certain occasions when they can't find a "missing-but-presumed-dead" person. She actually has a very high success rate (something close to 90%) when it comes to finding them. I guess she "sees dead people."

Unless you have developed similar skills, however, I would suggest that you probably can't read the minds of others—living OR dead.

Relationships—especially marriages—often get in trouble because one of the parties somehow thinks they can read minds.

"I saw you stare at that woman."

"What woman?"

"Oh, come on Howard, you KNOW what woman. The blonde with the great big thingies."

"I wasn't staring at her. I was staring at her car."

"Oh, really, what car was that?"

"Her 1966 Corvette 427 big block convertible in original Rally Red. That engine puts out 425 horsepower, you know."

"Howard, I can read your mind. You weren't thinking about the car . . . you were drooling over the driver."

"Oh, come on, Ethel! You know that I only have eyes for you . . . and 1966 Corvette 427 big block convertibles."

The thing is, Howard can't win in this situation. He will never prove that he wasn't staring at something other than the car. That's because Ethel believes that she can read Howard's mind. And because she's been married to him for thirty-seven years, she is fully aware how much he loves a woman's "thingies."

This can work in reverse, of course:

Ethel: "Howard, what would you like for dinner?"

Howard: "Whatever you want, dear."

So Ethel makes spinach-stuffed shell pasta, and sets a plate of it in front of Howard. He looks at it with disdain.

Howard: "You know that if we're having pasta, I'd prefer something with pesto."

Ethel: "Well, you know, Howard? You haven't mentioned that lately. And I can't read your mind, you know."

Oops, Ethel. What's going on here? One minute you can, the next minute you can't?

The "you can't read the minds of others" limitation of your powers goes beyond your spouse/partner/ significant other. It extends into the realms of your children, your coworkers, your teachers/professors, and your employer.

That's why workers often don't know that they will be the next to be laid-off. That's why people in advertising cannot declare with certainty which ad campaign will be the most effective. That's why sales people do not always know which person will buy and which one won't. There are too many unknown factors affecting each buyer's decision. Example: with cars, it could be color, style, price, cargo space, gas mileage, country of origin, number of seats, quality of the sound system, or recommendations of friends or *Consumer Reports*. And that's only the beginning of the list.

Admit it. Unless you are clairvoyant, *you* can't read minds, either. It's one of the thirteen "You Can'ts" that we all confront.

Here's the good news! For every You Can't, there is an "equal and opposite" YOU CAN!

You can communicate! (Openly and honestly.)

You can avoid making assumptions.

You can ask questions.

You can provide honest, straightforward answers.

And if you still get it wrong, you can apologize.

And the other party can forgive and forget.

It requires a certain measure of maturity to work through that process. But you're obviously mature. After all, you're reading this book!

two

You Can't Make Yourself Responsible for the Health of Others

have a friend I've known since 1976. That's a long time. Let's call him Gary (although his name is Dave).

For years, Gary/Dave has "accused" me of trying to be his surrogate father. "I already have a dad, and one is enough," he has reminded me.

Why does our long-time friendship have this strange dimension to it? Well, Gary is a heavy smoker and a heavy drinker, and, as his caring friend, I think he's killing himself. And that brings out the "dad" in me. I want my "son" to live.

When I say heavy smoker, I'm talking two packs a day. It used to be three packs or more, but at the price of butts these days, he's been forced to cut back. Not only that, but there are fewer public places where smoking is permitted, so it's tougher to smoke that many cigarettes . . . especially in public places.

Every time we get together—for business or purely social reasons—without warning, he will suddenly embark on a major coughing jag. I think he has COPD . . . or worse. He thinks that smoking is actually a healthy habit, mostly because he wants to believe that, and because some idiot rock star told him that is a fact. (He can't recall who that moron was. And I asked him as I was writing this.)

When I asked him about his smoking a few months ago, he sent me some ridiculous questionnaire that was a lame attempt to validate smoking to non-smokers. The correct answers were: 1) Car exhaust is worse, 2) Barbecue grills are worse, 3) Cell phone radiation is worse, 4) More people die while watching TV than while smoking, and, of course, 5) The government is lying.

But one of the thirteen "You Can'ts," of course, is "You Can't Make Yourself Responsible for the Health of Others." I just hope I don't have to watch Gary/Dave die. "Dad's" hate that stuff.

Here's another true story that is even more personal. And painful.

My own dad was not a smoker or a drinker, and, in fact, even in his seventies he exercised daily, ate healthy foods, and remained amazingly fit. But he abhorred medical doctors and avoided seeing them for years.

One Thanksgiving Day, after a wonderful dinner my mom and my wife had prepared, Dad and I went out for a walk . . . to, hopefully, lose the extra pounds we had just packed on at the dinner table. I noticed that occasionally he would hold his stomach and a look of pain would cross his face. I was concerned.

"Dad, are you feeling okay?"

"Yes, I'm fine."

"Have you had a physical lately?"

"Yes."

"Well? What did the doctor say?"

"Everything's fine."

"You sure?"

"Yes."

Here was this man who had taught my brother and me not to lie, yet everything he said was a total fabrication. He hadn't been to any kind of doctor in recent memory . . . except his dentist. He was a fanatic about his teeth. (That's because both of his parents had "falsies" that they kept in jars overnight . . . and he didn't want that outcome.)

The following Spring, he was admitted to the hospital with severe abdominal pains. Surgery revealed that he had advanced colon cancer. The surgeon removed everything he found to be cancerous, and closed him up.

We thought he'd be released from the hospital in a few days, but food simply wasn't moving through him. Every day, the nurses would listen to his tummy with stethoscopes. No gurgling noises. Not a sound of any kind.

The surgeon determined that Dad had likely developed post-surgical adhesions. So he opened Dad up again, and, sure enough, that was the problem. The doctor removed the adhesions, and Dad went home.

Memorial Day arrived, and Dad put on his VFW uniform, went out to the front yard and raised the flag, then asked Mom to drive him to Fort Snelling National Cemetery for the annual observance. She hesitantly agreed. It would be his last visit to the cemetery alive.

In August, he was having great difficulty with eating, so finally, over his objections, Mom drove him to the hospital again. I met her there and sat with her through an eight-hour surgery in which they removed more cancer. (No matter what was going on, my Mom was always thinking about others. In the middle of our long grueling wait, she asked me, "Have you sent Rosh Hashanah cards to your Jewish friends yet?" "No," I replied. "Have you?" "Of course," she said. "We do every year." So, of course, that was the beginning of a brand new tradition for the Christian son of Christian parents.)

When Dad was finally released, he was sent to a nursing home. He was only there a couple weeks when he was again rushed to the hospital. This time, the surgeon took one look, shook his head, closed him up, and came out to see my mom and me.

"I'm sorry, but the cancer has spread everywhere. There is nothing more I can do. I'd suggest you find somewhere to place Roger so he can live out his last days in comfort."

Seven days later, I went to a second nursing home to visit Dad. It was my seventh visit in seven days. When I saw him, I immediately slipped out into the hallway and called my kids—three of his five grandchildren. "If you want to see Grandpa alive again, I think you'll have to come today."

They all did. And my instinct was correct. He died that night. A few days later, he joined several of his World War II buddies at Fort Snelling. That day was his personal Memorial Day.

As I'm sure you realize, colon cancer is usually treated with a high degree of success when it's caught early. My dad was treated late. Very late. He didn't want his cancer to be caught early, I guess.

After the funeral, mom started going through Dad's personal papers. She found this note, written almost a full year before the first surgery: "For the past year and a half, indigestion has bothered me. Now the pains keep me awake . . ."

Two and a half years with cancer, and the only clue I had was when we went out for a walk after Thanksgiving dinner. And he said, "I'm fine . . ." while bent over in severe pain.

Some readers may argue that I could have done more to intervene in my father's health. But really, what difference could I have made? I didn't "own" him. It was one of life's "you can'ts."

Yes, there are some things you can do on behalf of the health and well-being of others.

You can be a positive example . . . especially to your children and other younger family members. Since my dad died, my brother, Dan, who is five years younger than I am, and I have colonoscopies every five years. We remind each other as our birthdays approach. If there is any disease in your family that seems to appear to be hereditary, this is what you do. You take precautions.

You can insist that the passengers who ride in your car wear their seatbelts. You can't enforce that when they are driving their own cars, but you can stop your own car and refuse to continue driving until they buckle up.

You can refuse to text or take calls on your cell phone while you are driving. And you can teach that to your kids by example. (Have you ever seen the last photos of those decapitated drivers who "just had to respond to this text" and looked down for only a fraction of a second when they apparently tried to take a shortcut under the trailer of an 18-wheeler? It'll make you sick.)

As a parent, **you can require your kids to wear bike helmets** when they pull their bikes out of your garage. But you can't control whether or not they continue to wear them when they are out of sight. And you can't require them to wear their helmets when they grow up and buy their first Harleys.

You can refuse to let friends smoke in your home or anywhere near you. If they insist on smoking, they might not be real friends after all.

One last reminder: you can set a good example in all of these situations by buckling up yourself, ignoring your cell phone, wearing helmets on your own bike or motorcycle, and quitting smoking.

In short, you can't be responsible for the health and welfare of others. But you are 100% responsible for the example you set.

AN UPDATE ON "GARY/DAVE"

Indeed, as I suspected, Gary/Dave was diagnosed with COPD, and he now has to be on oxygen continuously. He even has to carry a portable, battery-operated machine with him when he goes anywhere.

He paid "big bucks" to undergo Stem Cell Therapy, but, despite glowing promises, it appears to have accomplished nothing.

But, wisely, because he does not want to catch fire while using oxygen, he has quit smoking. I have to be honest and report honestly, that had *nothing* to do with me.

A TRAGIC "FINAL" UPDATE ON "GARY/DAVE"

Sadly, my friend of forty-four years, Gary/Dave died in October of 2020, of Congestive Heart Failure—at age sixty-nine. (Surprisingly, NOT of lung cancer, which was my fear for a long time.)

Dave's wife came home from work to find him not looking well at all. She took a fingertip reading of his oxygen level, and it was forty-nine, despite carrying oxygen with him 24/7. (95% + is normal.) Naturally, she called 911 and an ambulance rushed Dave to the hospital. That night in ER, he struggled to breathe, so they sedated him and put a tube down his throat. He died two days later.

And his "Surrogate Dad" cried.

three

You Can't Make Yourself Responsible for the Happiness of Others

This chapter could easily have been titled "You Can't Make Others Responsible for Your Happiness." Because you can't. But that's not exactly where this book is headed.

After all, Chapter One could have been titled "Others Can't Read Your Mind," and Chapter Two could have been "You Can't Make Others Responsible for Your Health."

This book, though, is about *letting go*. About accepting your own limitations. About abandoning others in order to save yourself.

I know that statement may come off as self-serving. "Save myself? Why would I want to do that? Am I not supposed to serve others?"

Here's the key to this discussion. When I feel that it is my job—my responsibility—to make other people "healthy, wealthy, and wise," and I don't succeed, that makes me a failure. My "can'ts" become my "didn'ts," and that somehow makes me feel guilty.

I personally believe that "guilt" and "shame" are the most destructive emotions that we can experience ... especially if we hold onto them.

I remember that when I was about five years old, my parents took me to a picnic area in Minnesota where we met my other relatives for a nice Sunday outing. All of a sudden, I had to pee. ("Go to the men's room," for you genteel folks.) But there was no men's room nearby—that I could see. And my pleas for relief were not attended to by the adults. So I unzipped behind a thick (I thought) pine tree and took care of my business.

My Aunt Ginny witnessed the entire event, and shouted, "I SEE you, Stevie." I nearly died. My Aunt had watched me pee. And she had told the entire known world. On top of that, I had NOT made her happy! (Her own son, my cousin, Jim, who was my age, would NEVER, EVER consider doing something like that!)

Shame. Guilt. It took me decades before I could pee behind another tree. And, since then, I have always made sure that it was a true "emergency," and I was completely alone.

So . . . Aunt Ginny was not happy. Amused, maybe, but not happy. I was not happy. Not amused, either.

As a result of that and other experiences, I spent the next . . . oh . . . fifteen or twenty or twenty-five years dedicating my life to making others happy. That was not my actual focus. Nor was it my true problem. My problem—and thus, my focus—was that I did NOT want to wet my pants. ESPECIALLY on those social occasions when my Aunt Ginny was present!

At school, I wanted to make my teachers happy. Didn't work. I still had a "C" average. Barely.

I wanted to make my coaches happy. Dropping balls and missing free throws and swinging wildly at pitches I should have hit didn't do it. I never even "lettered" in high school. (Okay, I lettered in "band." Big whoop. "One time at band camp." But my dad was the band director, so that counts about as much as peeing behind a pine tree.)

I wanted to make my "girlfriends" happy. Okay, I'm not going to go there. . . . (Nothing to report, anyway.)

My sad story is, the only person I didn't devote my time and attention to was me.

I have learned that the best way to make others happy is to make sure that I am happy myself.

And then along comes "love, marriage, and the baby carriage." (That obscure reference is about a rhyme that was popular in the 1940s and 1950s—another century. Never mind.)

The point is, your spouse/significant other may EXPECT you to make him/her happy. It could start as a desire. It might evolve into a demand. It may eventually turn into an ultimatum.

Your "dating" months or years likely go very smoothly, of course. "Make someone happy . . . make just one someone happy . . . and you will be happy, too." You're in love, and you do everything possible to demonstrate your love.

Then comes marriage . . . or a civil union . . . whatever it is for you. Job pressures often take over. Deciding what's for dinner becomes more challenging than what to wear to a special event. The roles—who does what—may need to be re-negotiated. Money can become a nasty point of contention.

Then . . . whoops! As a couple, you add to the family . . . whether through a pregnancy or adoption.

This "little person" comes along, and he/she is not exactly the "miracle baby" you expected. It's very demanding. It wakes you up in the middle of the night. It wants food. It wants its diaper changed. It wants to throw up on your clean clothes immediately before you are "scheduled" to walk out the door, take it to day care, and head for work. It doesn't care one diaper-full about your schedule.

Now, in case you haven't noticed (and that's highly unlikely), I am calling your little "Bungle Of Joy" IT. Yes, IT.

That's because these future people don't fully function as human beings until they are in their twenties or thirties. (Sometimes even later than that! Brain Studies have proven that.)

In those interim, intervening, in-between years, you—yes, YOU—are expected to provide for every shred of their happiness. Food, clothing, shelter, rides to everywhere, trophies for showing up at games in clean uniforms, education, a brand new used car, gas, insurance, a budget-killing wedding, and even a pre-planned funeral.

But, guess what? They're not happy. They won't suddenly become happy. They will just want more.

After a while, you decide, "I'm not happy."

So, Friend, guess what your REAL job is. It's to teach them how to be responsible for their OWN happiness. Yes, you read that really stupid, naïve, unrealistic sentence correctly. You can't make yourself responsible for the happiness of others. Or their success. Or their education. Or their marriage. Or their children. Oh, yes, if you have lots of money, you can be responsible for giving them money. But I'm sure you've heard this before: "Money does not buy happiness." Money, used wisely, can buy freedom, and freedom can contribute to happiness. That's it. Nothing more than that.

Now, here's the thing. The vital thing:

If you are in a long-term relationship (such as a marriage), your partner wants to be ecstatically happy . . . and is counting on you to make that happen.

If you are the child of aging parents, they, too, expect you to make them happy. ("Please stay with me and hold my hand while I die! It'll be FUN!")

If you're a boss—an employer—your employees want you to make them happy. Raises. Promotions. Vacations. Benefits. Company cars. Cash and valuable prizes.

And if you're an employee, your job, of course, is to make your boss happy. Arrive early. Leave late. Put in extra hours for free.

Finally, if you're a postal worker, just give up. Because NO ONE will ever be happy. Not your postmaster. Not postal workers. Not customers. Sorry. It's a fact of life in America.

So, friend, since it's not your job to make yourself responsible for the happiness of others, it then becomes your job to be responsible for your OWN happiness . . . and let your happiness spill over into the lives of others in your world.

LEARN TO . . .
- Be happy about who you are. Accept yourself!
- Be a happy person to be around. Make your positive attitude contagious. (This has LONG been my greatest challenge! My wife claims that "negativity" is my natural state. I keep telling her that it's inherited.)
- Accept and even welcome the gestures of others in your life who want to contribute to YOUR happiness. Learn how to receive with gratitude.
- Find ways to give back. Donate canned goods to a food bank. Volunteer to serve meals at a homeless shelter. Open a vein and give blood to the American Red Cross. Give of your time in support of Scouting, or Boys Clubs Girls Clubs, or Big Brothers Big Sisters. Giving is actually fun!

Yes, I know that the title of this chapter is "You Can't Make Yourself Responsible for the Happiness of Others." But you CAN make your world, your community, and your life so much better in so many small ways!

four

You Can't Give Your Children— Or Anyone Else— Everything They Want

When I was a kid growing up in Minneapolis, Pemberton, Chisago City, St. Paul, Buffalo Lake, Henderson, and Mountain Lake, (all in Minnesota, and all of them before I turned twelve—we moved a lot!) it didn't take me long to realize that my parents couldn't afford to give me everything my greedy little heart desired. (Such as "New-found Friends" I would know longer than a year or two.)

They didn't have much money, so they told me that if I really wanted something, I'd have to work for it. And that's what I did. I started selling "all-occasion greeting cards" door-to-door when I was nine—thanks to an ad for the Junior Sales Club of America that I spotted in *Boy's Life* magazine. (For those of you guys who were never Cub Scouts or Boy Scouts, that was their official magazine. It offered everything you could want at that age . . . stories, projects, puzzles, cartoons . . . and ads.)

I delivered newspapers door-to-door when I was eleven. And I went door-to-door offering to mow lawns or shovel sidewalks for a small amount of money.

All this so I could buy a microscope, a six-transistor radio, and a Gilbert-brand chemistry set. (I loved making stink bombs with that "marvel" in a tin box.)

But there was one thing that even I—with all my hard work—couldn't afford to buy. And that was a Kodak Brownie 8mm Movie Camera. It cost $25 back then.

Thankfully, I came up with an alternate plan. I decided to WIN IT!

One of my favorite shows on our 13-inch Admiral black and white TV was "T.N. Tatters" on Channel 5 in Minneapolis/St. Paul. T.N. was a "poor" clown in tattered clothes. He had a Wishing Well on his show, and we loyal little viewers could send in post cards on which we shared our wishes.

"Aha," I thought. "One little two-cent postcard to KSTP-TV, and that Kodak Brownie 8mm Movie Camera will be mine." Other kids wanted ponies, of course, but I knew that I'd prefer to take movies of ponies, rather than actually ride one.

If TNT drew my card, I knew he would read my name and announce my special wish to the well. If the water "got waves" and visibly moved, I would get my wish. My parents pointed out that no one ever got ponies, so a Kodak Brownie 8mm Movie Camera was probably unlikely, too. But they reminded me that if kids asked for a "Cootie" game (one of the show's sponsors), they always got their wish. They advised me, "Go for the Cootie!"

I would rush home from fourth grade every day to make sure I didn't miss the show. Sure enough, TNT drew my postcard, read my name, and repeated my wish to the Magic Well. The water didn't budge. Not at all. No movie camera for "little Stevie Gottry in Henderson, Minnesota."

The next day all the kids in school ridiculed me mercilessly, because they all knew how it worked. "You should have gone for the Cootie," they all chimed in.

I learned to live with my disappointment, but this whole story gets even worse.

A couple years after the T.N. Tatters nightmare, we moved to another small Minnesota town—Mountain Lake. Every Saturday night in this boring little burg, the fire siren on top of a tall tower would wail. That's how they normally summoned the members of the Volunteer Fire Department when there was a fire, but it was also how we knew it was time to be "present" for the weekly "Winner-Must-Be-Present" drawing for a "Valuable Prize."

One Saturday night, to my dismay, my fellow sixth grader Linda—"OH, NO, NOT LINDA!"—won the drawing for a Kodak Brownie 8mm Movie Camera. My first thought was, "What is a dumb girl ever going to do with a movie camera?" Think about it: there were no Jodie Foster or Kathryn Bigelow-type female film directors back then. But again, I learned how to live with my disappointment. (I also eventually learned to stop calling girls "dumb." But that's another story . . . .)

Here's my sort of a "happily after ever" ending to the story. Recently, I gave a speech at my Toastmasters Club titled "Go for the Cootie." At the end of the speech, I unveiled my "brand new" very old, very own Kodak Brownie 8mm Movie Camera, which I had just purchased at an antique store near me for—you guessed it—$25. I finally got my wish . . . but nowadays, I can't even buy film for it, and if I could, film and processing would be ridiculously expensive. Instead, I take my "movies" on my iPhone or iPad or Nikon DSLR, or an OSMO Pocket Camera, or a SONY 4K digital video camera. (I earned them all by myself!)

The point is, whether you work for something, or you try to win the lottery, you can't always get what you want. It might be helpful to teach that harsh reality to today's generation of kids. Instant gratification seems to be their expected way of life.

SOME UGLY REALITIES . . .

Not everything in life works like a video game. Your kids cannot push buttons or download "cheats" to get to the "next level" of real life. A well-trained pair of thumbs won't do much for kids in real life. It's much more complicated than that.

Not everything works like a kid's Sports Team. My youngest daughter (who graduated from law school) played soccer and basketball as a kid. Whether she scored goals or blocked shots or led her team in scoring—or not—she received a trophy at the end of the season. The coaches (all of them really nice people!) would say incredibly nice things to each girl when the trophies were handed out. "You always came to practice." Or, "You always smiled at practice." Or, "Your uniform was always clean—even at practice!"

It can be a sad thing later in life when a kid discovers that "showing up and smiling, even in a clean uniform," is not enough. All of a sudden, grades, and college admission, and jobs, and promotions, and raises, are based on performance. Scary!

Here are the realities:

All things are NOT equal. And, believe it or not, this notion doesn't even work in Communist/Socialist countries—which is why so many of them "want out." Education, hard work, smart decisions, and a positive outlook make more of a difference than anything else. The way to BE equal is to THINK equal. Kids today need MENTORS more than they need MONEY. And the mentors are out there . . . and available. In fact, I'd bet that you could become a mentor yourself! What a wonderful way to give back!

There are too many "Joneses" in the world! You can't possibly keep up with all of them. The minute you think you've kept up with the Joneses who live next door, NEW Joneses will move in, put in an Olympic-size swimming pool and hot tub, add a new room, and install new granite countertops in their state-of-the-art kitchen.

Cash and Credit are two different things. Cash is the money you DO have. Credit is the money you DON'T have. It's the money you THINK you will have in the future.

The availability of easy credit has convinced people that there really is a T.N. Tatters Wishing Well . . . that you can have everything you want without delay. Credit cards are actually a despicable enemy to most people, unless those people are able to pay off the balance every month. Credit cards are the primary reason why financial gurus including Suze Orman and David Ramsey are so successful. Credit cards enable instant gratification but destroy financial futures.

The 10/10/10/70 Principle makes perfect sense. Most financial advisors, including my friend, Sharon Lechter, co-author of *Rich Dad Poor Dad* and other books in the *Rich Dad Series*, as well as founder of YOUTH-preneur (an organization that teaches financial principles to young people), believes and teaches that long-term financial success is based on this principle.

Here is a quick summary:

The First 10, means that 10% of your income (after taxes), should go to **SAVINGS**. This is the money you set aside to meet immediate, unexpected needs. It is your "nest egg" or "rainy day fund." It is immediately available to you if you lose your job, or have an unexpected car repair, or have to fly to some other city for— God forbid—an illness or a funeral.

The Second 10 is the 10% that you set aside for **INVESTMENTS**. This is an account (or accounts), such as an IRA, a Roth IRA, or a 401K, in which you "store" money away over the long term. This is money for your retirement. Tragically, many people do not plan for retirement until they are nearly ready to retire.

So, if you are under 40, you might want to consider that you might outlive your motorcycle and set aside for the retirement you cannot yet begin to comprehend. (Just sayin'.) This money should not be in accounts from which you can easily borrow. And, by the way, I am an advocate of putting some of this money into whole life insurance policies with a quality company. (I have long-used Northwestern Mutual Life . . . and no, they are not compensating me for endorsing them.)

The Third 10 is what you set aside for **GIVING**. I was raised in a very religious home, and this concept was known as TITHING. But you do not have to be a "person of faith" to give to charities—to worthy causes. Bill Gates, the founder of Microsoft, openly admits that religion is not "his thing." But he is giving away his billions without hesitation. (Okay, I am really not sure that I agree with all the causes to which Bill and ex-wife Linda are giving their billions, but that's not up to me. NOT telling rich people how, when, and to whom to give their money is on my expanded list of YOU CANT'S.)

Teaching your children about giving is a vital component of making our world a better place in the years ahead!

I'm sure that you already know what the *Final 70%* is for. That's the part of your income that you live on. Your **LIVING EXPENSES**.

But think about the people you know. How many of them skip the 10% Savings, skip the 10% Investments, skip the 10% Giving, and live on the 100% that remains—PLUS another 10, 15, or 20%? After all, the government (meaning City, County, State, and Federal governments) continually spends more money than it takes in. So it must work? Right?

No, it doesn't. It can't. Someone will have to pay for this philosophy. It could be you. It could be your kids. It could be your grandchildren. Or THEIR grandchildren. Spending more than your income does not work.

On the other hand, I know some scrooges who scrimp and save and deny themselves and their families of every pleasure in life—even the simple ones. They don't travel, they don't dine out, they don't go to ballgames or plays or concerts. They don't spend money on clothes or furniture or much of anything else. Of course, they're not broke, either.

So, what, in my opinion, is the answer? It's called BALANCE.

Balance means that you follow the 10-10-10-70 guideline, and don't twist it into 30-30-0-40, or some other imbalanced formula.

Balance means that you give your children what they need, but you don't feel obligated to give them everything they want. And you certainly don't go into debt to fulfill those wants. (One exception may be paying for their education, but if you've followed the 10-10-10-70 plan, you shouldn't have to borrow excessively to pay for tuition. Yes, I know college costs increase every year!)

Balance means that you teach your children that education, and ideas, and work, and helping others are all key ingredients of a successful life.

Balance means that you learn to prioritize. Determine what the really important things are in your life, and in your children's lives, and focus on them.

It could even mean that you avoid "binge buying, collecting, or hoarding. I know people who follow every new fashion trend, and fill their closets with the "quickly-outdated," rather than seeking out timeless styles.

It may even mean that you sell those things that you don't need or aren't using. This is also known as "decluttering," and it can be a really solid habit to establish in your life! (I should probably get rid of that Kodak Brownie 8mm Movie Camera. No matter how cool it looks on the shelf in my home office.)

five

You Can't Teach Others What They Don't Want To Learn

ven though I have taught English and Journalism at the college level, I'm obviously not an expert on education. But I believe that there are three things that impact an individual's ability to learn: *Aptitude, Attitude,* and *Interest.* I know this from personal experience as much as anything.

My parents extolled the virtues of education the entire time my younger brother and I were growing up in all those small towns in Minnesota. It wasn't just empty words, either; our family history supported the notion of education. My dad's mother, Elma Thomas Gottry, graduated from a small college in Indiana in 1909. (That was eleven years before women obtained the right to vote!) My dad worked hard to put himself though a private university in St. Paul, Minnesota, before he joined the U.S. Navy in World War II. Then, after the war, he earned his Masters Degree from the University of Minnesota.

Of course, I had different ideas. I announced at dinner one night that I was going to "skip" college and become a "drayman." (That's a garbage man who drives a truck and picks up trash, in case you didn't know that sixties term.) They essentially responded with, "Over our cold, lifeless bodies!" (Years later, I pointed out that huge amounts of money were to be made in trash collection, as evidenced by Waste Management and other successful companies. In the interim, of course, I graduated from college. I was given no other choice.)

Part of my objection to education was based on the fact that I had no interest in certain classes. History seemed useless to me. (I enjoy it now, though!) Latin was something that challenged me, and I had no interest in, or aptitude for, math. I also had a bad attitude toward numbers and formulas—an attitude that has survived to this day.

My dad tried valiantly to help me overcome my "arithmatic issues." We would sit for hours at the dining room table with a deck of playing cards, (no face cards) working on multiplication tables. I would throw down one card, and he would put another card down next to it, and I'd have to shout out the correct answer before he could count to three. If I succeeded, I would get the cards. If I failed, he would take the cards. The person with the most cards obviously won. I hated that game.

In junior high, I nearly failed beginning algebra. Then, a year later, I excelled in geometry—because it was more "visual"—but the following year, I dropped out of Higher Algebra in favor of an English Composition class. I never took trigonometry or calculus, and I honestly have not done one algebra problem since ninth grade. Ever.

When I got to the University of Minnesota, my first challenge was dealing with the required classes that didn't interest me—Spanish, Biology, History, and others. Fortunately, there were no required math classes, but Spanish proved to be a formidable nemesis. My Spanish 1 teacher sent my grade on a postcard from Mexico during our winter break. All it said was, "Feliz Navidad! F." Nice.

Despite the hassles, I ultimately graduated with two degrees and started a business that I operated for more than twenty-three years.

I actually can see the value of education, and I support school issues in every bond election. As I noted previously, I even taught upper division college-level English and Journalism at a Phoenix-based University.

I enjoyed this tremendously, because my students all possessed and demonstrated three key traits: Aptitude, Attitude, and Interest. They had developed their skills, they had positive attitudes, and they were interested in what I was teaching. It was wonderful!

But what if they had not possessed any writing skills, hated being in class, and were so disinterested that there was no chance they'd learn anything? In that case, in my opinion, they would have been in the wrong place at the wrong time for all the wrong reasons.

Which brings me to a key point. Parents (and school counselors) often do kids a disservice by encouraging (and sometimes demanding) that they go to college. If those kids do not have a suitable aptitude, a positive attitude, and a high level of interest, they are wasting their time and money and may never become fully engaged in their future careers.

There are other options. There are junior colleges, trade schools, and, of course, there is the military. I have friends, for example, who have put their mechanical aptitudes and interests to work as aircraft mechanics, NASCAR team members, and machinists or welders. I have other friends who have served in the military and have then become outstanding, decorated police officers or highly proficient computer technicians. They learned all the skills they needed in the military.

Square pegs have never fit in round holes—and vice versa—and that's not going to start happening now, just because you tell a kid that's what YOU expect, or that's what a kid should expect and demand of himself or herself.

And, yes, there are lots of studies that demonstrate that people with college educations earn more than those with high school diplomas. And those with post-graduate degrees—MS, MA, or Ph.D.—are likely to earn even more.

If money is the primary goal—if making more of it trumps happiness and contentment—then college may be the answer.

But if you decide to place your emphasis on doing something you actually love for most of your life, a trade school can be a viable and desirable alternative.

In the city where we have lived for more than twenty-four years, there is a well-established school known as EVIT: The East Valley Institute of Technology. Their course offerings are so diverse that a potential student would have to be fully "checked out of life" to be unable to find a field of learning that does not interest him or her! Want to pursue Broadcasting? Go for it! Have the desire to be a Chef? That goal can be reached! Have you thought about becoming a welder or machinist? Lucky you! The world needs more people with these skills.

My belief is that any interested, involved student in any school—technical, trade, or whatever—can become successful by learning how to be creative ... how to innovate. AND by learning how to manage the money they earn.

I am glad I went to college after all. Garbage stinks. And driving a truck day after day would not have satisfied my need to be creative. But there are others for whom that is the perfect job. Allow them the freedom to pursue the path they choose!

six

You Can't Say "Yes" to Every Request from Everyone

Chances are, you have a friend, a relative, or a coworker who is a "People Pleaser." This person is unable to say "no" to anyone or anything. Serve on my committee? Sure. Drive me to the store? You bet. Loan me some money? Of course.

Hopefully, you are not that person. You may think your purpose in life is to make others happy, but chances are you will be making yourself miserable. And you're also making other people dependent on you, rather than helping them do things on their own.

There are several reasons why people become "Yes-Men" and "Yes-Women."

Some follow that path because they want to become "indispensible" to others. It also goes by the name "feeling needed."

Others do it because they want to be loved.

Still others want to avoid hurting feelings.

The worst-case scenario, though, is the reality that some people say yes to anyone and everyone who asks them anything and everything because they have no actual lives of their own. They don't have their own goals, dreams, or engaging projects, so they make themselves available to help others achieve their goals, reach their dreams, or complete their projects.

I am not advocating becoming a selfish jerk who never offers a helping hand. But it's far better and usually more productive that you respond with a "Yes" to those requests for help on things that truly interest you.

That means, of course, that you have to prioritize both your personal life and your charitable life.

Start by ranking these people in your life. Simply assign numbers indicating where each person/persons fits in. Then, say "Yes" to the top five, and "No" to the bottom five.

☐ Partner

☐ Children

☐ Parents

☐ Grandchildren

☐ Siblings
☐ Best friend(s)
☐ Your nieces and nephews
☐ Your employer
☐ Your in-laws
☐ Your neighbors
☐ Your co-workers
☐ Your "club"

There! That was easy, wasn't it? Especially since I practically thought it through for you!

Yet, no matter who or what is in your top five, you can't possibly say "Yes" to every request. So, then you have to prioritize by the *type* of request.

☐ Health, welfare, safety
☐ Financial need
☐ Help with household chores
☐ Help with moving
☐ Help with cleaning, painting, decorating
☐ Temporary housing
☐ Temporary transportation
☐ Or simply being a good listener!

Using our daughter as an example, if she needs a ride to the hospital, saying "yes" would be at the top of my list. When she needs help moving or painting her new apartment, I am quick to volunteer. If she needs money for medications, yes; if it's money for a pleasure trip to New York, no. If she wants me to clean her oven, I plan to have other plans. (Unless it looks as though it is about to catch fire, of course.)

The good thing is, the smartest people in your life will know which type of request will elicit a "yes," and which ones will likely get a "no."

It's also important to prioritize your areas of charitable involvement . . . along with the time and money it takes to be involved.

How would you rank these possibilities?

- ☐ Human/Physical needs. The Homeless, Homeless Shelters, Food Banks, Missions.
- ☐ Domestic Animal Protection and Welfare. (Shelters, etc.)
- ☐ Wildlife Causes.
- ☐ The Environment. Conservation ("Green") Efforts.
- ☐ Youth Organizations: Big Brothers Big Sisters, Boys Clubs Girls Clubs, Boy Scouts, Girl Scouts.
- ☐ Youth Sports: Soccer, Little League, Pop Warner Football, Volleyball, Hockey.
- ☐ Social Issues: Pro Life, Pro Choice, LGBTQ.
- ☐ Elder/End-of-Life Concerns, Hospice Volunteering.
- ☐ Political: Campaigning, Fundraising, Running for Elected Office.
- ☐ Religious: Teaching Sunday School, Vacation Bible School, etc.

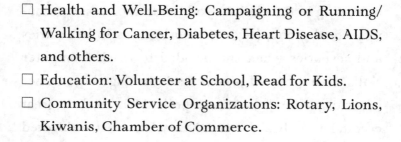

☐ Health and Well-Being: Campaigning or Running/ Walking for Cancer, Diabetes, Heart Disease, AIDS, and others.

☐ Education: Volunteer at School, Read for Kids.

☐ Community Service Organizations: Rotary, Lions, Kiwanis, Chamber of Commerce.

Naturally, there are a number of ways to contribute. The four main ways are TIME, TREASURE (Money), TALENT, and TOUCH. (This idea is not original with me. I borrowed it from *The Generosity Factor*, a 2002 book by Dr. Ken Blanchard and S. Truett Cathy, the founder of Chick-fil-A.)

TIME means that you run in marathons, raise money to support your participation in your events, serve meals at a homeless shelter, volunteer for your local Boys Club Girls Club, or help clean up a city park or a stretch of highway. Of course, you have to prioritize.

TREASURE means that you give money. But unless you are "ultra rich," you can't say "Yes" to everyone. So, again, you have to prioritize.

TALENT simply means giving of those things you do well. If you are a skilled carpenter, electrician, or plumber, you may decide to give back to Habitat for Humanity, or an organization that works to rehab blighted urban areas. Or it could be something as basic as singing in the choir at your church or in a community vocal group. (My own mother was in her sixties and seventies when she decided to teach "computer skills" to a group of pre-teen and teenage boys at her inner-city church in Minneapolis, MN. To their great credit, I never heard even ONE racist, sexist, or bigoted comment out of the mouths of either my mom or dad!)

TOUCH means that you may visit a nursing home or hospice and offer comfort. Even though I'm not Jewish, I used to grab my Tanakh (Jewish Bible), put on my Yarmulke (that little skull cap thingy) and go to the hospice to read the Psalms of King David to a close friend from my Toastmasters group. He loved it. He appreciated that "touch." His son asked me, "Are you Jewish?" I said, "No, I just love your dad." Richard had touched my life in so many ways. All I wanted to do, as he was dying, was "touch" him back.

Here's the bottom line: when it comes to saying "Yes," your spouse/partner, kids, and parents should come first. After that, you need to give yourself "permission" to prioritize other people and requests based on your time and treasure considerations.

In other words, don't "bankrupt yourself" because of an overwhelming, uncontrolled desire to say "Yes" to everyone. "Just Say No."

seven

You Can't Answer Every Question Asked of You

When asked a question, the most difficult thing most people could possibly say when they respond is "I don't know."

Saying "I don't know" is like admitting we're imperfect, stupid, or less than "all knowing."

Saying "I don't know" is as though we are admitting that we are somehow flawed.

The obvious truth is, you can't possibly know everything, so you can't answer every question that is asked of you. You are not Google, DuckDuckGo, or Wikipedia. And, honestly, those websites can't answer the daily, contemporary, immediate, relevant questions we all face. Such as, "What time will you be home for dinner?"—in the midst of a work project with a tight deadline.

For me, this "can't" began when I realized that I didn't always know the answer to every true/false or multiple choice question on every test in junior high, high school, or college. That led to a lot of average grades, or course. (If I really didn't know the correct answer, I would choose Answer "C." I got it right roughly one-fourth of the time.)

My understanding of the "can't" was amplified when I got a job in the so-called real world. "What would be the best solution to this problem?" Quite often, I simply didn't know.

Then, of course, I got married. Spouses generally think that they are married either to an encyclopedia or a clairvoyant. I frequently get asked to instantly convert ounces to milliliters, or kilometers to feet, yards, or miles . . . or vice versa. Another good one (especially when I meet an "attractive" woman for the first time) is, "How old do you think she is?" (Hint: anything less than eighty-five or ninety is the wrong answer.)

And then I became a parent. All of a sudden, two little people (and, eventually, three) were following me around the house, asking all the difficult questions. (You haven't *LIVED* until your four-year-old asks, "Where do babies come from?")

Here's one thing I *DO* know, however.

It's "OKAY" not to know.

Of course, you can always make something up . . . kind of like Fake News. The problem is, if you are found out, you will lose credibility.

These days, with "Smart Phones," we are all nearly always connected, and most of the answers are within easy reach.

But if you don't know the answer and can't readily find it, do yourself and others a favor . . . and admit it!

Along the same line, I also believe it is okay to respond, "I don't know the answer to your question for sure, but here's what I THINK it could be, based on my experiences (or what I've read)." At the very least, this response demonstrates that you have interest in the discussion.

Think about how you would respond to these questions—whether you think you have an answer or admit that you don't.

1. Why do bad things happen to good people?
2. Why do serious diseases, such as cancer, come into some people's lives . . . and never impact others?
3. Why do people, tribes, and nations fight wars?
4. Why do different races exist? (And why do they struggle to get along?)
5. Why are there such awful things in the world, including Child Abuse and Human Trafficking?

6. What are some of the reasons why so many marriages end in divorce?

7. Why do people adopt behaviors and habits that
have the potential to destroy their lives? (In this
category, I include smoking, drinking, drugs, addi-
tive legal medications, over-eating, pornography,
reckless speeding, texting while driving, and gam-
bling. I'm sure there are many more.)

Perhaps if you can answer some or most, or all of
these questions, you will contribute to a safer, kinder,
smarter, more-secure, less-troubled world!

In the meantime, don't get all stressed out if you
discover that you can't supply all the answers to the
more typical, routine, everyday questions in life.

eight

You Can't Achieve Every Goal, Desire, Or Dream

When I was in grade school, I dreamed of being Superman. You already know the sad outcome of my "Cape and Undies" project.

When I was in junior high, I wanted to be an Astronaut. I listened on the radio as Alan Shepard became the first U.S. man in space—on a fifteen-minute suborbital flight. I listened to the radio again as John Glenn orbited the earth three times before he splashed down in his tiny capsule. I even skipped school in order to listen to the launches and splashdowns. (It wasn't until much later—1969—when NASA landed on the moon—that I watched it all "Live" on television. THAT would have been a wonderful experience! But, by then, I had given up on my dream.)

When I was a high school senior, I wanted to be President of the United States. I thought I would be a good one. I try to be fair. I care about the poor, but I also care about not spending more money than we take in. I have a big heart, I love our country and our Constitution, and, while I dislike war, I understand that threats must be met with strength.

In college, I clearly and completely revised my dreams. Instead of becoming an astronaut or president, I decided I would start my own advertising agency. So I did. I achieved that dream. And it worked for me for twenty-three years.

Here are the three key things about dreams:

1. They change over time, so you will need to adapt.
2. You probably can achieve SOME of your dreams.
3. But you likely won't achieve ALL of them.

As a result, you need to sort out your dreams—your goals. If you think about it, there are only five types of dreams. In this case, we will call them goals. Because, as many leaders and inspirational speakers have pointed out, "A Dream is a Goal with a Deadline." (I actually first heard this statement from Dr. Marjorie Blanchard, founder of "The Office of the Future" at The Ken Blanchard Companies in Southern California.)

In terms of goals, I believe there are five basic types:

1. Realistic Goals

These are the goals you will most likely be able to achieve, based on your inherent or carefully developed skills, underlying interests, education, and deep desire. If you don't really want something and you don't work toward it, you are most likely not even going to come close.

For example, I have never wanted to build, plumb, and wire my own house, so I never have. On the other hand, my talented son-in-law-the-engineer, really wanted to do that, so he did. Fortunately, my eldest daughter aligned herself with his vision, and she helped every step of the way. Now, they and my granddaughter live in a 3,000 square foot "cabin" on a beautiful lake in Northern Minnesota. (I don't fully understand the "Lake in Minnesota" thing—it's cold up there!)—but I sure enjoy visiting them and watching the sunset over the sparkling cold water. (Yes, they fish, and I don't.)

2. Unrealistic Goals

We have already established that I have not designed, built, plumbed, or wired my own house. I leave that to smart sons-in-law. As for me, I simply don't have the inherent or carefully developed skills, underlying interests, education, or deep desire. Building a house (or even a shack) would have been my personal unrealistic goal.

3. Goals you can train to achieve.

Somewhere along the line, I developed an interest in flying. No, not like Superman, but in an actual airplane. So, because I knew something about the principles of aviation, had an interest, was willing to learn, and had the desire, I earned my private pilot's license (in my own airplane) from Dave Johnson, a great instructor who then went on to be a Delta Airlines pilot and instructor for Commercial Pilots.

I went on to earn my Instrument Rating, instructed by Ms. Terry Lynch, another competent, caring flight instructor. I achieved this goal in my second airplane, that was bought and paid for by Clint Eastwood. (But he doesn't know that, and it's a story for another time. Sadly, I never met the man, and I admire him tremendously.)

The wonderful thing about both of these gifted flight instructors is that they taught me that even lowly private pilots need to "Think and Act like Professionals." Training was everything. In flying, there are no shortcuts to staying alive and protecting your passengers. It's the same reason you don't (or shouldn't) text while driving. Or drink and drive.

Because I had a growing advertising business at the time, the airplanes I owned helped me reach and be of benefit to those clients who were in other cities: Dallas, Des Moines, Topeka, Cincinnati, Chicago, Fort Wayne, and Milwaukee . . . among others. And I didn't have to mess around with airline schedules, although I flew on Commercial Airlines to Los Angeles and San Francisco. Those are long trips. Over mountain ranges. With downdrafts. No thank you!

4. Goals you have sought and achieved.

For me, of course, these goals include graduating from the University of Minnesota; starting my own ad agency and video production company; leaving cold, frozen, over-taxed Minnesota for the (much) warmer weather of Arizona; and buying a house with a pool in the back yard. I also include my goal of coauthoring a book with one of my personal "author heroes," Dr. Ken Blanchard.

To some extent, even short-term impulsive goals can count, and they can bring unexpected joy into your life. An example: one beautiful evening, Karla and I had dinner at a Minneapolis restaurant known as First Street Station. It was situated near a railroad switchyard, so after dinner, we spotted a train engine on a nearby track. "Let's ask the engineer if we can hop a ride." He likely violated every company safety rule, as well as their liability insurance policy, when he said "Yes." But we gleefully climbed into the cab of the engine with him, and we watched as he skillfully moved various box cars and flat cars into the correct positions around the switchyard. It was, as they say, "A Night to Remember!"

5. Un-reached goals.

I don't consider un-reached goals to be impossible goals. They may simply be impractical or illogical.

One quick example: after I earned my private pilot's license and instrument rating, I decided to pursue my "multi-engine" rating. This would mean that I could fly faster, higher, in more comfort, and with a greater payload (weight). I took a couple of lessons and had my eye on a Cessna 340 RAM twin-engine aircraft. It had more seats, more navigation "goodies," (I am a sucker for technology), was faster than my Piper Arrow IV, had De-icing equipment (important in Minnesota!) and it had a pressurized cabin, so it could fly above much more of the really bad weather. On top of all that, the price was right!

But that was about the time that things in my businesses turned sour. For a wide range of reasons, I lost tons of money, had to close my office, and was forced to sell my toys—cars, boat, aircraft hangar, and, of course, my airplane. Naturally, this major event also made sense to forego multi-engine flight training, and abandon my dream of a Cessna 340 RAM.

My simple point is, it's okay to eliminate or revise a goal when it becomes impractical or less desirable/less prudent.

You certainly do not need to feel as though you have failed. I don't . . . even though I don't own a hangar with a twin-engine Cessna, Piper, or Beechcraft in it. Or a Boeing 777!

One More Big Thing:

When building your list of dreams and goals, you will benefit from being as realistic as your present situation dictates.

The three main considerations are your age, your physical abilities, and any limitations imposed by finances. The harsh reality is that money (or LACK of money) really DOES erase many dreams and goals. But age and physical ability (and even innate talent) come into play, too.

Here is a partial list of my personal examples:

1. I love football—especially the NFL! (I was thrilled and honored to help the great Rosey Grier develop his autobiographical book, *Life Through Rosey-Colored*

Glasses. If you are old enough, you may remember Rosey as part of the "Fearsome Foursome" of the Los Angeles Rams, or as the brave hero who wrestled the gun out of the hands of Robert F. Kennedy's assassin at a political rally back in 1968.)

But, as much as I love football, there is no way a dream of becoming a linebacker, or wide receiver, or quarterback could ever become a reality. I simply don't have the size, the speed, or the skill. Plus, no one of my age has ever been drafted by an NFL team. EVER!

2. I would not even DARE walk onto a golf course with Phil Mickelson or Tiger Woods. If you ever witnessed my horrific slice for yourself, you would understand instantly. Every drive would "take out" at least one innocent person in the gallery.

3. Even the seemingly simple things in life evade me. Some people have "green thumbs" and can get any plant to grow. I, on the other hand, have a "black thumb." I can kill Astroturf. That's why the front yard of our desert home in Phoenix is covered with rocks and bricks.

Yes, I Have Some Closing Thoughts For This Chapter:

I firmly believe in having goals, desires, and dreams. They are an essential part of a fruitful, meaningful, and memorable life. Part of your significance. I don't want to die with regrets: "I wish I would have

_____."

There is a "but," however. It's truly okay to have BIG DREAMS and GOALS. My friend and coauthor on other books, Mark Victor Hansen, is one of those inspiring people who refers to them as BHAGs: "Big, Hairy, Audacious Goals." These are the goals that motivate us and compel us to strive for more than we ever imagined possible.

The "but" is that you need to have the raw DRIVE to pursue those goals. "Quitters" need not apply.

You also need to develop the ability to ask others for help. The aforementioned Mark Victor Hansen, and his wife, Crystal Dwyer Hansen, fully explain this principle in their 2020 book, *ASK! The Bridge from Your Dreams to Your Destiny.*

TIMING is also important! There is always a right time and a wrong time to pursue any goal, venture, idea, or dream.

So, pick the RIGHT TIME, the PERFECT GOAL, and GO FOR IT!

nine

You Can't Instill Goals, Desires, or Dreams In Others

Everyone's Goals, Desires, and Dreams belong to them alone. Just as your goals, desires, and dreams belong solely to you.

The underlying reason, of course, is simple. We all have different interests, aptitudes, attitudes, and priorities. We are all unique human beings. Ones of a kind!

Much of the difference is related to our unique personality type. Some of us are extroverts. Others are introverts. Some of us make decisions and set our priorities based on our logical thoughts. Others make decisions based on our feelings . . . or intuition. Some of us learn much through our environments . . . home, school, social groups, and so on.

But, in our society, parents often expect their kids to achieve things in which those kids have ZERO interest. (I'm sure you know what's coming next. Yes, a personal story.)

When I was about seven or eight, living in a small, rural town in Minnesota, my dad noticed something about me. I was tall for my age. (In fact, when I graduated from high school, I was six-feet, four-inches tall. And only weighed 145 pounds. Go figure! I was not an appealing sight, that's for sure!)

So, at seven or eight, my parents said, "We're signing you up for youth basketball. You're tall—you'll LOVE it!"

I DID *NOT* LOVE IT. Every Saturday, I had to walk a few blocks to our small school, change into "gym clothes" in a stinky locker room, and shoot hoops. Over and over. And dribble and pass, naturally. On top of all that, I was no good at it. Any of it. (Except the walk back home when it was over!)

Here's a tidbit that likely won't resonate with ANY of you. This happened so long ago that the Los Angeles Lakers were, at the time, the "Minneapolis Lakers." And the huge stars of that era were George Mikan and Vern Mikkelsen. For some reason, my dad knew them, and invited them to come to our local small town basketball clinic to "inspire us." I was not impressed. (I WAS impressed years later, when I met Mr. Mikkelsen at a sports banquet at the Decathlon Athletic Club in Bloomington, Minnesota. He was truly a wonderful guy! He did not remember me, though. And, no, I never saw Mr. Mikan again.)

With basketball clearly behind me, my mom thought I should take up ice skating. In Minnesota. In the winter. Outdoors. Who invented this stupid activity, anyway? So, every winter, I sat inside the "Warming House" and talked with the other kids who also thought skating was "stupid."

What did I want to do? Well, in seventh grade, some friends and I thought it would be fun to build rockets. (Some of them were more like pipe bombs, actually.) My mom said, "This doesn't really sound safe to me." We assured her that it was completely safe. It wasn't. My buddies and I could point out some ill-placed shrapnel to prove it.

Yes, I have another example. And, yes, it is a personal story.

My son, my eldest adult child, basically struggled with school. When he graduated from high school, he had no idea what he really wanted to do. Because my great-grandfather and grandfather had printshops and were newspaper owners in Northern Minnesota—and because I had friends who worked in the printing business and made good money operating printing presses, I suggested, "Jon, you're mechanically minded. Why not attend vocational school and take up printing? Printing presses are mechanical!"

So, he did. Did he hate it? Of course, he did. "Ink stinks, Dad." Is Jon a printer today? You're kidding, right?

Naturally, this experience was the inspiration of this chapter.

So, readers, three kids later, have I succeeded in instilling ANY goals in their lives? I really don't know. But if this book turns out to be a hit, they may go on "Oprah" or some other TV show, and tell you the actual truth. ("We call it 'Our Lying Dad's Stupid Book.'")

My simple point is, "LIVE your OWN life." Let others live their own lives, too. YOUR Goals, Desires, or Dreams are not likely to inspire or change others.

ten

You Can't Take Someone Else's Place In Life . . . Or Death

eath is a heartbreaker. It doesn't really matter whether or not you have faith, or believe in heaven and eternal life. Death is pain.

It's especially painful for a parent who loses a child to a devastating illness or a horrible accident. That's not right. Death is "supposed" to happen in a certain order: grandparents first, then parents, then children, and finally grandchildren. (You should NOT be around for the grandchildren.)

My earliest memory of death was when I was twelve, and my "Grandpa Cholesterol" died of a sudden heart attack at age sixty-seven. I posthumously gave him his nickname because he loved cheese (he lived in Minnesota fewer than twenty-five miles from the Wisconsin border!), and he also loved to grill big thick steaks. (He often advised me, "Eat the fat; it's the best part." I didn't, and still don't.) His passing was a brutal experience.

My second encounter with death was when a sixteen-year-old classmate apparently committed suicide. (I say "apparently," because there were several, unexplained circumstances surrounding his death.) His passing was even more brutal and shocking.

But, in terms of "brutal and shocking," the worst for me was my cousin (one of only two first cousins in the world), who died of Leukemia when I was nineteen, and he was only fifteen, going on sixteen. Naturally, I have lost several more friends and relatives—before and after my cousin—but this was especially heart-breaking.

Chuck was young, healthy, and vibrant—a high school track star known as "Flash." One week he was feeling great, the next week he was admitted to the Mayo Clinic in Rochester, Minnesota, and a week later, he was gone. I was appointed to be one of six pall-bearers at his funeral. I could not believe how HEAVY a teenager could be. It must have been the extra weight of grief.

ENOUGH with my personal stories! The point of this chapter is that I COULD NOT have taken the place of any of them either in life or in death.

Here is a pathetic honest confession about me. I wouldn't willingly take ANY of their places in death, either. You may think that is the most selfish thought you have ever heard from anyone.

But I consider myself to be a "Judeo-Christian." My Christian beliefs tell me that "It is appointed unto men once to die." (Hebrews 9:27)

Thankfully, it is NOT my task to carry out that assignment, nor to schedule the appointments. But I DO believe that God knows when "the end" is going to happen.

And, as far as I know, my beliefs also tell me that only one human being in history has ever taken my place in death.

As a Christian with strong roots in Judaism, I believe that Jesus Christ did that about 2,000 years ago, not only for me, but for all of humanity. I'm certainly not asking—nor do I expect—you to believe the same way I do. This is not intended to be a book about Christianity or Judaism or another faith of any kind. But I know for an absolute fact that countless numbers of my friends and associates—be they rich or poor, educated or not, young or old, male or female, of every race and nation—believe the same way I do. Perhaps it is because of this statement by Jesus himself, found in the biblical book of John (Chapter 15, Verse 13): *"There is no greater love than to lay down one's life for one's friends."*

I'm fairly certain that there are some people for whom most of us would willingly give our lives ... likely our spouse and children, and possibly even a sibling or other close relative. And over the years, many servicemen and women have thrown their bodies on live grenades to save the lives of their military brothers and sisters. But, unless you have enlisted in the Secret Service and taken their official oath, you might not be willing to "take a bullet" for the president or any other politician. (Or an entertainer or sports figure, for that matter.)

Years ago, I met a wonderful Dutch woman named Corrie ten Boom. She was the author (with John and Elizabeth Sherrill) of a bestselling book titled *The Hiding Place*. (It was also made into a movie of the same name: my small marketing firm created the posters and other promotional materials for the motion picture. This was such an honor for me ... sometimes I can't even believe that I had the opportunity to spend time with this remarkable woman of sacrifice and faith.)

Corrie, her sister, her father, and several other members of this close-knit family were willing to risk their lives to save the lives of their Jewish friends and neighbors—along with others they had never met—when the Nazis invaded Holland in World War II. All but Corrie died, either before imprisonment, or while enslaved in a concentration camp.

It was a demonstration of courage. Of love. Corrie may not have actually taken the place of others in death. The point is, she was willing to!

Most of us will never have such an opportunity . . . or be confronted with such a difficult decision.

Right at this moment, I am thinking about the Shepard Boy of Centuries ago, named David, who was asked to face and fight a giant of a man known as Goliath, armed with only a slingshot and small smooth stones. The Giant went down in defeat, and David became a great king and leader. (His son, Solomon, became one of the wisest and richest leaders of history.) King David, and Corrie ten Boom both exemplify the wonderful trait of "bravery."

Think about it. For whom would you be willing to die? Or, if asked, would you simply respond, "You're on your own."

eleven

You Can't Love Everyone

Face the facts. Some people are simply unlovable. And, my feeling is, most unlovable people don't try all that hard to be loveable.

What are some of the factors that contribute to certain people being more "lovable" than others? Why are they "easier" to love?

Of course, I have my own opinions on this matter. (Having my own opinions and being able to state them is one of the benefits of being the author of this book!)

1. They smell good! Meaning they shower often, they use scented liquid sprays (cologne or perfume) but NOT too much, they wash their clothes, and they brush their teeth and use mouthwash.

2. They don't argue about *everything*. (That doesn't mean they are pushovers . . . they simply "pick their battles." They are not petty.)

3. They are generous. They are not stingy with their time, their money, or their talent. If they know how to drive, they use their ability and their time to deliver meals to needy families who may not have transportation. (Yes, simple things really make a difference!)

4. They LISTEN more than they TALK.

On the other hand, there are people I WISH I could love, but they are constantly setting up "road blocks." They continuously build walls, and post signs on those walls that say "do not enter."

Example: I recall driving from Phoenix to Las Vegas, and we needed to make a "potty stop." Since there was no nearby Pine Tree that Aunt Ginny could peek though, we pulled into a large gas station/visitor's center in this small, obscure town on our route. The huge sign above the main entrance read, "VISITOR'S WELCOME."

But when we got to the door, there was a smaller sign that read, "NO BUSSES." Thankfully, we had arrived in a car, so their "roadblock" did not apply to us. (There was a long line in this "Middle-of-nowhere-bathroom," though.)

But what about the poor folks who arrived in Greyhounds or charter buses? Were they expected to search for pine trees, and hope that Aunt Ginny was nowhere nearby?

RULE MAKERS are on my list of unlovable people—especially if those rules are basically arbitrary.

SELFISH PEOPLE also make my list. Have you ever really watched kids (even the very young ones) play with one another? They grab toys out of the hands of other kids and announce, "That's MINE!" It begins at a very early age, and often gets progressively worse over time.

PROUD, BRAGGY PEOPLE aren't all that easy to love. I know rich people who only talk about their money, their possessions, and their wealthy friends. One guy I know is not only incurably proud of his $100,000+ huge Mercedes SUV loaded with all the toys and gadgets. But he also posts pictures and stories on his Facebook page CONSTANTLY, about of him using his expensive vehicle to haul gifts and food to homeless people in a small, poor village in Mexico. (That's a good thing, actually, but his way of "promoting himself" reminds me of this principle I learned as a young teenager—it's kind of long, and yes, it's another idea from the Bible . . . this time from the beginning of Matthew 6.)

Here it is from *The Message* version:

"When you do something for someone else, don't call attention to yourself. You've seen them in action, I'm sure—'playactors' I call them—treating prayer meeting and street corner alike as a stage, acting compassionate as long as someone is watching, playing to the crowds. They get applause, true, but that's all they get. When you help someone out, don't think about how it looks. Just do it—quietly and unobtrusively."

Another version suggests this thought,

"But when you give to the needy, do not let your left hand know what your right hand is doing, so that your giving may be in secret."

—Matthew 6:3–4 (New International Version)

The basic idea here is that *PRIDE* and *BRAGGING* really don't make anyone look all that selfless. I think of those as unlovable human characteristics.

CONTROLLING PEOPLE comprise another group that isn't always that easy to get along with. Everyone knows someone (or more than one) who is eager to tell you what to do, how to act, or what to think. They would be more than willing to manage your time, your money, and your relationships. But this control is usually to their benefit . . . not to yours.

CONTROLLERS employ a variety of techniques to exercise their control. Some use Guilt or Emotional Blackmail—"If you really love me, you will do this or that." Others use their time and attention. Some use sex, and those with money will often use their wealth, or perceived wealth. Example: a sibling or parent with money will sometimes seek to control vacation destinations for the rest of the family.

Loveable people tend to be givers rather than takers, listeners rather than talkers, and more forgiving than most people. They love as deeply as they hope to be loved. You *want* to be around them, rather than do everything you possibly can to avoid them.

But are you *expected* to love everyone? Of course not! However, you can treat everyone—even the unlovable—with kindness and respect. We all deserve that!

twelve

You Can't Make Someone Else Love You

ove is everywhere! Love, and its counterpart in some respects—sex—are the subject of most books, movies, television program, and songs.

Think about it. The Beach Boys wrote songs about loving cars, beaches, surfing, and girls. The Beatles declared, *All You Need Is Love*. Shakespeare wrote about the dark side of young love in *Romeo and Juliet*. *Love Story* was an enormously popular book and movie in the 1970s. More recently, love and sex have taken on *Fifty Shades of Grey*.

But there are several older views of love. One is from the New Testament, found in the book of First Corinthians:

"If I could speak all the languages of earth and of angels, but didn't love others, I would only be a noisy gong or a clanging cymbal.

"If I had the gift of prophecy, and if I understood all of God's secret plans and possessed all knowledge, and if I had such faith that I could move mountains, but didn't love others, I would be nothing.

"If I gave everything I have to the poor and even sacrificed my body, I could boast about it; but if I didn't love others, I would have gained nothing.

"Love is patient and kind. Love is not jealous or boastful or proud or rude. It does not demand its own way. It is not irritable, and it keeps no record of being wronged.

"It does not rejoice about injustice but rejoices whenever the truth wins out. Love never gives up, never loses faith, is always hopeful, and endures through every circumstance."

—I Corinthians 13: 1-7 (New Living Translation)

Those words represent a very high standard that is beyond my reach—and possibly yours. But it certainly poses some interesting ideas!

You Can't Buy Love.

There's a great book titled *The Five Love Languages* by an author named Gary D. Chapman. I'm not going to spoil it for you by telling you what the five languages are; you need to read the book for yourself.

But I need to make an important point here. Unless you are communicating to your partner using the language he/she most values and understands, and unless he/she is communicating with you in the language you most value and understand, you're NOT really communicating.

Many people, I believe, misunderstand the purpose behind communication in the ideal love language. They somehow think that they can influence/cause/bring about "love." That they can make someone else love them.

When I was young and naïve, (now I'm old and naïve) I was in love—or so I thought—with an attractive young lady who was a year behind me in high school. (I'd mention her by name, but she's married to a professional wrestler.)

I guess I never figured out what *her* preferred love language was, so I attempted to express my feelings for her in the one language I thought I understood: Giving Gifts.

So, one Christmas, I stopped by her house with what was probably close to fifteen presents, and left them with her parents. They tried to place them under their Christmas tree, but they didn't all fit. So the rest of them went to the basement game room.

Was she impressed? No, that little ingrate was actually embarrassed. She saw my expression of love as excessive, as unnecessary, as totally silly. Our "relationship," such as it was, basically ended right about then and there. Fortunately, I later married someone who understood and appreciated the "language of gifts." (The problem is, I currently don't have the cash to buy them.)

I sincerely suggest that you read Gary Chapman's book. It will probably save you time and money, and possibly spare you from some pain.

You Can't Buy Friends, Either.

This thought runs parallel to the main point of this chapter: "You Can't Make Someone Else Love You."

For several years, I owned a boat in Minnesota that was "perfect" for entertaining. So, naturally, I entertained.

I served lots of food to my clients, suppliers, and staff, and gave them a tour of the resplendent homes on the lake. There were times when there were up to twenty or twenty-two people on board. And because the boat was powered by twin Chrysler 318 inboard engines, food wasn't my only expense. Fuel costs were right up there.

With a couple of notable exceptions, I would have to admit that the people I entertained were not my friends. They wouldn't "go the extra mile" for me. If I were dying in some hospital and needed transfusions, I doubt they would have given blood. Some of them were blatant back-stabbers and wished me ill. They certainly never helped with cleanup after a five-hour cruise.

The difficult lesson I learned is that I couldn't "buy" friends. (Any more than I could buy the love and affection of "Miss High School.") So sad that it took a thirty-foot boat with a flybridge and an amazing stereo sound system (and a huge stack of Christmas gifts) to learn that!

Stalking Your Beloved Does Not Work.

I have two friends—a man and a woman—whom I have known for many years. I have been in occasional contact with them, and have seen them in person several times . . . but not together. What I was not aware of was the fact that the guy (who is married) has a major "thing" for the woman. He has been "pestering" her on social media and through emails and phone calls. In fact, I would consider it to be "stalking." (He admitted to this.)

One day a few years ago, she emailed me and said, "You know him well, if I recall. Would you mind talking to him and telling him that I am just not interested? Even if he were single and lived next door to me, I STILL wouldn't be interested."

So, I did exactly that. But I haven't talked to either one of them since, so I don't know what happened. I don't know if it was ever resolved. (I think he was upset with her for telling me, and I turned out to be the Messenger he wanted to Shoot. Or perhaps they are living "happily ever after." Together or not. Who knows?

Love Is Both Objective And Subjective.

"Subjective" means that you are attracted to another human being's appearance, personality, intelligence, beliefs, or even money. And that is basically why you love that person. (Or THINK that you do.)

"Objective" means that your opinions (or statements) are unbiased or "fact-based." You love your twin children Roberta and Robert, because they are your children . . . not because they are cute, funny, smart, or because of any other factor or trait. Your love is unbiased and based on the obvious facts.

Love often begins with subjective information (appearance, personality, or bank account value), but, over time, love may more fully develop, and it becomes more objective. After all, looks can fade, weight gain sometimes occurs, personalities can change under the stresses of life, and cash in the bank can be used up. NOTHING is FOR SURE or FOREVER . . . unless it's the thirteen "You Can'ts" (and that could grow to be a list of fifteen, seventeen, twenty-one or more).

My personal belief is that as wonderful, poetic, beautiful, mystical, and important love is, love can actually be broken down and understood in two basic categories.

This is so basic—so simple—that perhaps I should be punished for actually discussing it. Yet, there just might be a couple of readers out there who don't yet know this basic fact. The ONLY TWO KINDS OF LOVE are:

1. CONDITIONAL LOVE,
   and
2. UNCONDITIONAL LOVE.

Conditional Love is often all about "Me, me, me." ("I will love you if there is something in it for me.")

Unconditional Love is all about, "You, you, you." ("I will love you no matter what! Even if you hurt me.")

Conditional Love may help explain why there have been so many unwanted babies and terminated pregnancies over the years. The male in the relationship says something like, "If you *REALLY* love me, you would *PROVE* it to me!" And far too many young ladies have fallen for that unbelievably selfish reasoning.

Unconditional Love explains why even the most disappointed parent will always love the selfish, spoiled child. If you have never read the story of the Runaway,

Disrespectful Son and his Loving, Forgiving Father in the Bible, here it is, from THE MESSAGE version (Luke 15:11-24):

"There was once a man who had two sons. The younger said to his father, 'Father, I want right now what's coming to me.'

"So the father divided the property between them. It wasn't long before the younger son packed his bags and left for a distant country. There, undisciplined and dissipated, he wasted everything he had. After he had gone through all his money, there was a bad famine all through that country and he began to hurt. He signed on with a citizen there who assigned him to his fields to slop the pigs. He was so hungry he would have eaten the corncobs in the pig slop, but no one would give him any.

"That brought him to his senses. He said, 'All those farmhands working for my father sit down to three meals a day, and here I am starving to death. I'm going back to my father. I'll say to him, Father, I've sinned against God, I've sinned before you; I don't deserve to be called your son. Take me on as a hired hand.' He got right up and went home to his father.

"When he was still a long way off, his father saw him. His heart pounding, he ran out, embraced him, and kissed him. The son started his speech: 'Father, I've sinned against God, I've sinned before you; I don't deserve to be called your son ever again.'

"But the father wasn't listening. He was calling to the servants, 'Quick. Bring a clean set of clothes and dress him. Put the family ring on his finger and sandals on his feet. Then get a grain-fed heifer and roast it. We're going to feast! We're going to have a wonderful time! My son is here—given up for dead and now alive! Given up for lost and now found!' And they began to have a wonderful time."

The truth is, you can't make anyone love you unconditionally. And you can't make anyone love you conditionally, either.

An Exercise in understanding LOVE in your life.

List the people whom you love conditionally or subjectively. (Perhaps you like the way they look, act, or think.)

1. _____
2. _____
3. _____
4. _____
5. _____
6. _____
7. _____

Now, list the people you love unconditionally or objectively. (You may want to begin with your parents, children, and siblings . . . and, hopefully, your spouse.)

1. _____
2. _____

3. _____

4. _____

5. _____

6. _____

7. _____

I hope you actually did this exercise. And I also hope it enlightened you a little and you enjoyed it!

Here are the words I wrote several years ago . . . by which I actually try to live my life. (I admit that it's not always easy to do.) This is what is framed and hangs on the wall in my home office. I can see it right now, while I am sitting here writing this book . . . .

A WAY OF LIFE . . .

L Learn Something New Every Day!
Laugh Every Chance You Get!

O Order Your Goals and Priorities!
Offer Help and Encouragement to Others!

V Value Your Relationships!
Value Yourself!

E Enjoy Every Day!
Expect the Best!

thirteen

You Can't Love Others Without Loving Yourself

On the previous page, you will notice that one of the key points under the "V" in "LOVE" is "Value Yourself." By that, I mean, "Love Yourself." And I honestly believe you cannot truly love others unless you first love yourself.

This concept is probably the most misunderstood aspect of love. And understanding it is still one of my most basic struggles.

By now—the last numbered chapter—you are convinced that there are certain things you CAN'T accomplish. But I believe you can love who you are.

Of course, by now, you are likely convinced that "Ol' Steve" is NOT a psychologist, psychiatrist, life coach, or social worker. I am simply an old guy (nearly an antique) doing my best to dispense the best advice I've absorbed in my life.

When you think of someone "loving themselves," the first thoughts that come to mind might be egotism or narcissism. But self-love (or self-respect or self-acceptance, if self-love is too strong of a term for you) is far from being the same as ego or narcissism.

In fact, I'm guessing that you've heard this old teaching: "Love your neighbor as much as you love yourself."

This is part of the answer Jesus gave to one of the many questions asked him by the religious leaders of his time. Here it is (in context) in the book of Matthew in the Gospels: Matthew 22:36–40 (the Living Bible version):

"Sir, which is the most important command in the laws of Moses?

"Jesus replied, 'Love the Lord your God with all your heart, soul, and mind.'

"This is the first and greatest commandment. The second most important is similar: 'Love your neighbor as much as you love yourself.'"

That wise instruction is first found in the biblical book of Leviticus, 19:18, in the Orthodox Jewish Bible:

"Thou shalt not avenge, nor bear any grudge against the bnei ammecha (children of thy people), v'ahavta

l're'acha kamocha (but thou shalt love thy neighbor as thyself): I am Hashem (the LORD.)"
—Vayikra 19:18

I firmly believe in the Commandments and laws as delivered to the Prophet/Leader Moses thousands of years ago. I believe that they provide the strongest foundation any society or civilization could have!

As a result of my thinking about the Commandments, I believe that it is not only clear that it is okay that you "love yourself," but it is also expected. I believe that loving yourself makes it more possible and likely that you will love your neighbor. Since the Bible also gives strong clues as to the identity of your actual neighbors, that means that it is important to demonstrate your love.

How do you do that? By feeding the poor. Sheltering the homeless. Visiting prisoners and the ill. Helping the disabled.

Imagine how much better the world would be if we all did our part . . . to whatever extent we are able. No one can do it ALL, but we can all contribute!

For many of us, "Loving our neighbors as ourselves" may also mean taking a stand against racism, anti-Semitism, or sexism . . . or any of the other negative "isms."

So, I have some thoughts on how, exactly, to "love yourself. " (Of course, you knew this was coming!)

1. Change—or TRY to change—your worst personal attributes into better ones. (This may require BRUTAL HONESTY, or even outside help—professional counseling, an Intervention, a spiritual advisor, or possibly even safe medications. Personally, I believe that there are LOTS of HUGELY unsafe medications out there.)

    Please be aware the even SMALL changes can make a big difference . . . if you are open to change. Every change you make in your life does not need to be monumental.

2. Realize . . . and accept . . . that you are not perfect, and never will be. The good (or maybe bad) news is that no one else is perfect, either.

3. Forgive your parents . . . or other ancestors. Most of them did the best they could. Of course, they ALL had flaws. But, the ability to forgive is often seen as a true sign of maturity. Are there things in my life that I regret . . . that I wish I could erase or change? Of course! Do my parents, my wife, and my three "kids" wish that I could change those things? Of course they do.

I tend to be a "list-maker." If you share that trait, consider making two lists:

LIST ONE: Things about myself that I am happiest about. This list will give you permission to love and accept yourself.

LIST TWO: Areas about my life that I would like to change—or be WILLING to change. (Of course, this list shouldn't include any "You Cant's.")

Didn't make those lists? PLEASE DON'T scold yourself. After all, you are NOT your "Aunt Ginny."

Epilogue

Moving Forward Now That You Know This

hope this book has convinced you that—just because there are certain things you nor anyone else can do—you still may not be everything that you *could* be! When it comes to the needs and desires of other people in your life, you are probably doing all you can, within reason, to help them. My guess is that you say "yes," more often than you say "no."

But remember, you can often do more to help someone by saying "no." A NO can help them GROW. It can make them more self-sufficient. More self-reliant. More resilient.

Now, because I have some wonderful friends who have previewed this book in its pre-publication form, I can guess what many of you are thinking:

"Okay, I understand the basic idea behind the 'YOU CAN'TS,' but why did you choose the thirteen specific ones that you wrote about in this book? Certainly, there must be many additional ones that you could write about."

Yes, of course there are. Here are a few that come to mind immediately:

1. You can't convince someone to change their strongly-held political views based on your brilliant Facebook or LinkedIN or Instagram post.

2. You can't force someone who hates to eat green peas to suddenly devour huge bowls of them. (I would be that "pea-hater.")

3. You can't persuade someone to become your lifelong closest friend against his or her will.

Naturally, there are MANY more.

The reason that I chose the specific ones I wrote about are because they address some of the most basic issues in life—especially relationships, health, parenting, and your personal goals, dreams, and desires.

If I somehow missed an area that you are thinking about, you are free to mention it to me. Just email me at gottry@mac.com. Or you can also send me a letter:

Steve Gottry

Priority Multimedia Group, Inc.

P.O. Box 41540

Mesa, AZ 85274-1540

Acknowledgments

I LOVE this part of every book I write, because it gives me a rare opportunity to express my appreciation and gratitude for those special people who have most impacted my life. Of course, I can't mention all of them by name, but be assured that, if I know you, YOU are a part of this wonderful group!

First of all, of course, I have to thank my wife (since 1984), Karla, who somehow acquired or developed the patience to tolerate a writer who interrupts her thoughts to scribble a note about his own thoughts!

I am blessed with three wonderful kids, Jon, Michelle, and Kalla Paige (who are now all adults), as well as a brilliant son-in-law, Jared, and my beautiful grand-daughter, Hallie Grace. (I call her "Princess Grace.")

I learned so much from my late parents, Helen and Roger Gottry, that I can't even begin to list it all. And I am STILL learning mountains from my only sibling, my younger brother Dan. He is the bravest man with the strongest faith I have ever known, as he continues to battle cancer for the third time ... with the faithful support of his wife, Sandy, and his two sons and their families! (I have never heard a negative word out of Dan's mouth!)

My High School English teachers, Ole Loing, Dorothy Tweet, and Bertha Olson, gave me the kinds of writing assignments in which I could get engrossed—despite the fact that none of them could teach me how to diagram a sentence. (They all tried.)

Nonetheless, I have employed everything I have learned to coauthor the series of "SPEED WRITE" books on writing, screenwriting, editing, and publishing with "Mr. Chicken Soup," Mark Victor Hanson, the all-time *New York Times* bestselling author, with more than 500 million books sold. Naturally, I am grateful and honored to work with him.

I owe a great debt of gratitude to Dr. Ken Blanchard (co-author of *The One Minute Manager* and co-author of our book, *The On-Time, On-Target Manager*). In addition to ghostwriting and editing a number of other books on his behalf, Ken also referred me to his wife, Dr. Marjorie Blanchard, his son, Scott Blanchard, NFL Legend, good friend, and needlepoint expert Rosey Grier, and the brilliant Michael Gerber of *"E-MYTH"* fame—for whom I have completed several projects.

As a follower of the" Judeo-Christian" tradition, I must acknowledge my two beloved Rabbis, David and Daniel Lapin (brothers), and my "wise-beyond-his-years" Pastor, Riccardo Stewart, a one-time star of the Arizona State University football program. (Yes, football is my favorite sport . . . but also nothing I would ever play.)

(And once again, Steve over-acknowledges . . . it's just too much fun.)

I am grateful for the friendship of my best high school buddy, Jack Janzen, as well as my lifelong friends, Father Duane Pederson, and the late David Gjerness (my extraordinary graphic designer for many decades), the late Tom Cousins (my boss at WCCO-TV), the late Tom Tipton (my boss at TCOIC), the late Dr. Leonard Bart (my favorite professor at the University of Minnesota), and the late Don Stolz (long-time owner, producer, and director of THE OLD LOG THEATRE.) I am so sad that so many of my friends are "late."

Finally, I want to thank my agent, Dan Strutzel, and my publisher, G & D Media, NY. Okay, I'm finished. Oh, Wait! Clint Miller and Pam and Gary Benoit.

About the Author

Steve Gottry is a Minnesota born-and-raised author, ghostwriter, screenwriter, playwright, and teacher who has lived in his "chosen state" of Arizona (as opposed to the "frozen state" of Minnesota) since 1996.

He founded Gottry Communications Group in 1970. This Minneapolis-based advertising agency served a variety of clients, including Alpha Video, HarperCollinsPublishers, NewTek, Warner Bros. Distributing, World Wide Pictures, and the Prudential Realty Group. His team won many prestigious local and international awards, and the firm was named "Small Company of the Year" by the Bloomington, MN, Chamber of Commerce in 1991.

Steve is the author of *Common Sense Business*, and the coauthor, with Dr. Ken Blanchard, of the bestseller, *The On-Time, On-Target Manager.*

He teamed up with Mark Victor Hansen (co-creator and co-author of the *Chicken Soup for the Soul* Series) to create a mini-series of books on writing, known as Speed-Write books. (For example, one of the titles is *Speed Write Your First Screenplay.*) The books are largely based on the curriculum Steve created for an upper-level English course ("Writing as a Career") that he taught at Grand Canyon University in Phoenix.

As a ghostwriter, he has worked with the late Chick-fil-A founder S. Truett Cathy, with "E-Myth" guru Michael Gerber, and several other authors, including ghostwriting the autobiography of NFL legend Rosey Grier. He recently ghosted *The Authenticity Factor* for Dr, Sharon Lamm-Hartman.

Steve is also a screenwriter with four produced children's movies to his credit. One of them—*The Story of Jesus for Children*—has been dubbed into 176 languages and has been seen by nearly a billion people worldwide.

He has written and produced an award-winning video for UMOM New Day Centers, a group of Phoenix homeless shelters. He also serves on the board of directors of Hands of Hope, which aids the homeless, prisoners, and runaway teens.

Steve is a current Toastmaster and a former Rotarian (Paul Harris Fellow).

He is married to Karla, and is the father of three adult children (Jon, Michelle, and Kalla Paige), and the grandfather of Michelle and her husband Jared's daughter, Hallie Grace.